WINTER

WINTER

=

Patrick Lane

COTEAU

Cover: stone-cut, 1959, "Bird Dream Forewarning Blizzards" by Tudlik. Reproduced with permission of the West Baffin Eskimo Co-operative Ltd., Cape Dorset, N.W.T. Photograph courtesy of the Art Gallery of Ontario.

Back cover: photograph of Patrick Lane by Brenda Pelkey.

Edited by Anne Szumigalski.

Typeset by Lines and Letters.

Printed and bound in Canada by Hignell Printing Ltd.

The publisher gratefully acknowledges the financial assistance of the Saskatchewan Arts Board, the Canada Council and the Department of Communications.

Canadian Cataloguing in Publication Data

Lane, Patrick, 1939-

Winter

Poems.
ISBN 1-55050-002-3 (pbk.) — 1-55050-003-1 (bound)

I. Title.

PS8523.A53W55 1990   C811'.54   C90-097022-7
PR9199.3.L35W55 1990

C O T E A U   B O O K S
Suite 401 – 2206 Dewdney Avenue
Regina, Saskatchewan
Canada S4R 1H3

This book is dedicated
to the memory of:
Milton Acorn,
Gwendolyn MacEwen
b p nichol,
and Bronwen Wallace.

sitting perfectly
still
and only
remotely human

Phyllis Webb

Winter 1

The generosity of snow, the way it forgives
transgression, filling in the many betrayals
and leaving the world
exactly as it was. Imagine a man
walking endlessly and finding his tracks,
knowing he has gone in a circle. Imagine
his disappointment. See how he strikes out again
in a new direction, hoping this way
will lead him out. Imagine how much
happier he will be this time with the wind
all around him, the wind filling in his tracks.

He is thinking of that man,
of what keeps him going.
The thought of snow,
small white grains sifting
into the holes where his feet went,
filling things in,
leaving no room for despair.

Winter 2

In the album he holds in his thin hands
are the thousand photographs he has made of winter.
Each one is perfectly exposed, each one a pure
white with sometimes only the barest of shadows;
a fleeting, ephemeral grey that betrays
the image of who or what it was he took.
It pleases him to go through it slowly and remember.

Winter 3

It will be winter when they come.
He will sit with his back to the high window
and imagine their tracks in the snow, the circles
and arabesques, the sudden turns, the fallen angels.
He will follow them to the end of their tracks.
He hopes it will not be where the ice ends.
He hopes it will be in the centre
where they have mounded the snow.

When he arrives he will wait for a storm.
Surrounded by crystals
he will peer down their breathing hole
smelling the sweet simplicity of their mouths
deep in the blue cavern where they sleep
and then
he will take his spear
and thrust it through fold after fold of snow
holding it there while they twist
just below him in the cold.

Winter 4

He is thinking of the end of Oedipus,
not the beginning, not the part
where Oedipus chooses by giving the answer
to the beast at the crossroads. No,
it is the end he likes. The part
just after he puts out his eyes
and stands, suddenly
in that certain darkness, decided.

It is not a story of winter
but of the sun, the ceaseless
perfection of the desert in Africa.

How different it would be
had it taken place here, he thinks.
Here the critical moment
would be putting the eyes back
in their sockets, that first shock
exactly the same as in the other story
only the beginning would have
to be different, all the roles
reversed.

Winter 5

The sound of winter is made up of all
the things not there. That is what *north* means,
to remember by forgetting everything. It is
precisely the same as someone
knocking on the door with a tentative fist.
It is almost delicate, muffled by leather and wool,
a muted sound he does not hear, perfectly.

Winter 6

The guests have arrived at last. The old
woman in rags who pushes a steel cage
filled with her life, and the man with dogs,
the two pit bulls who whine with eagerness
at the end of their tethers. The young boy
with the burns on his face and shoulders
stands by the piano where the girl with no legs
plays early Mozart, one of the pieces
full of promise composed when he was still
a child. There is wine and fruit and fine brandy.
Everything is ready to begin.

The host is sitting in his study, staring
at a painting from the Ming Dynasty.
Soon he will go down the long white stairs
and join them, but for now he is simply happy,
the painting one of winter, so much
like the porcelain of the period, pale,
with only the faintest of green
buried beneath the pure hard surface.

Winter 7

It is the bare bone of winter
he holds in his hand, a wisp of ice
slender as a fifteenth century Spanish knife
fashioned in Cordova. A woman's knife
to be hidden in a sleeve when meeting
a false lover. It is delicately curved,
a small floating rib, just right
to slip into the heart as they embrace.
He looks at the thing in his hand
as it transforms itself, changing,
melting into a thin pool of water. He is
almost afraid to return it to its element.

Winter 8

The second riddle is more difficult.
The answer to the first riddle was *snow*.
Not the soft snow of early winter, but
the coarse granular snow that sweeps
with the wind in the blizzards of January.
The kind that leaves the skin
scored with myriad tiny cuts.
The answer to the second riddle
could be *snow* as well. He
repeats the enigma to himself,
pondering the last couplet:

The absence of colour
is the colour of blue.

For a moment he wonders if the answer is *love*.
Perhaps it is *ice*.
Or it could be *cold*, that simple word
for which there are a thousand meanings,
all of them correct.

Winter 9

Each day the time grows less, the hours
shorter by a few minutes, the sun
farther away. He remembers the Inca,
the way they would tie
a rope to the sun and hitch it to stone
out of fear it would never return.
How strange to think of their songs,
the supplications, the hearts torn out,
the blood on the altars. What wonder
must they have known as they lay
their bodies on stone? How simple
their desire, the priests chanting,
the sun drifting farther and farther
north. But not now. For him it is winter
and for them the sun is returning.
He sees them singing on the terraces
as they plant the young corn,
their children waiting for the season
when they are chosen, the one that begins
when everything starts to end.

How beautiful, he thinks, gazing
from his window at the night, this darkness
gathering in the blue snow.

Winter 10

Standing under the dark spruce trees,
their branches bent under the weight of snow,
he watches the people enter The Sacred Heart
just before midnight, just before mass
when they celebrate the birth, the
beginning of light, the promise
things will get better. He likes
to listen to their singing, the voices
of the young children, and the women.
What he likes most is to watch
them as they leave and enter
the storm that has risen while they prayed.
How they pull their coats
tight around them, the mothers
sheltering their children, the fathers
staring at the night just before
leading them away. The small
moment of doubt in their eyes.
He likes to stare at the priest
standing behind them, the one
who touches with great gentleness
the choir boys in the sanctuary.
The priest is full of hope and fear,
knowing they are leaving with his words
in their minds: All that singing
and still no end in sight.

Winter 11

He reaches down and strokes the white fur.
Each day the animal grows larger. He wonders
at the cells multiplying beside him,
duplicating and reduplicating themselves
without end. Somewhere in the animal heart
there is a single cell which has begun
it all. He wonders what it looks like now,
grown grotesque with the myriad others
surrounding it, weighing it down,
their wild impossible crying for more.

If that is the first cell, he thinks,
then what is the last? He reaches out,
pulls one hair from the animal's throat.
He breaks off the base where it is still
a pure white and swallows it.
This is what it is like,
all these choices without refusal,
only waiting to see if you are right.
He feels the animal beside him, its heaviness.
He thinks: *Later when it tries to remember*
I will point to the snow.

Winter 12

The magpies wait in the bare tree.
They cry out for the dead.

There is no food
in this place where nothing moves.

This is what he likes. All this hunger
and nowhere to hide.

Winter 13

There is a brief thaw and now
everything is frozen. Outside
ptarmigan wander ceaselessly
trying to find a way back
to where they believe
there is release from cold.
Beneath them their white sisters
struggle under the clear crust.
In the rare moments
when they are still
they are mirrors of each other,
each of them dying, each of them
wanting the other's dilemma,
believing the cries of the others
are lies, something done
only to torment them.

Winter 14

The moon arrives just before the clouds,
hard and bright in the sky. The hunger moon.

So much time. So little patience.
The snowy owl sleeps on his pole in the garden.

Winter 15

Fragility and nowhere to go.
So many questions. Like
where do the snakes go?
What he wants is
stillness, absolute zero
when everything becomes
the same, perfectly still,
waiting. Fragility, like
the snakes know as
temperatures fall, their
bodies getting colder
and colder. So many questions,
as in *what?* or *where?*
Or resemblance, that word
like making it all possible,
fragility and snakes,
the night dragging on.

Winter 16

Everything moves without change. The trees
without leaves dance sadly, allowing
nothing to get in their way. Not sorrow,
not snow under snow, but a slow forgetting.
The old moon sleeps with the young moon in her arms.
Words like that are like reaching out
in the darkness, wanting
to sleep and not being able to. Reaching out
to find nothing at the end of the hand but cold.
Wondering at flesh, its need, as the trees
who do not remember leaves, dance sadly
with a steady dumb grief, their dark moving
a monotonous music in the snowy night.

Winter 17

The stones in the thin winter months
melt what little snow stays on their backs,
melt and pull the spare water beneath them
where it freezes, lifting them
higher where the wind cuts them,
reducing them to dust, a single mote of which
has blown into his eye, blinding him,
making him see through the sudden tears
a world made for one moment entirely of water.

Winter 18

Naked in the empty room
the young girl offers herself. Such a forlorn gift,
such a hopeless dance; so incomplete
with only innocence to offer. Her love, so awkward
without wantonness, leaves him
with two possibilities: *transgression* or *transformation*.
A simple defeat.
How he makes himself holy in order to suffer loss.
If there is anything in him
resembling love
it is for the two white pom-poms on her socks
which is all she wears on this cold floor
as she moves around him,
so much like the snows of early fall.

Winter 19

His tears quickly freeze, forming
delicate icicles on the pale hairs of his lip.
If he stands perfectly still in the wind
he can breathe their small impossible music.

Winter 20

Winter is not Colville, not that violent sentiment
without feeling, control without grief.
He is not how we imagine it. We are not
his model of intolerance, that accuracy
which is performance designed to instruct.
Imagine the space in falling snow
left behind by a woman
when she is walking through a storm.
We think it chaos,
but it is only presence reduced to intrusion.
Another order, which is what he praises.
It is soapstone before the carver
lifts his chisel, the form before form,
desolation without regret. Propriety
in a space made alien by the thought.
The answer to the question:
But what does it mean?
The old Eskimo laughing at such a strange request.

Winter 21

To be under ice in the dark is just
one more way to believe, as a fish must who leaps
from water in the wrong season, suddenly
finding no way out. To relinquish movement.
That kind of decorum, the one
without imagination,
the one the Japanese have, their tradition being
the repetitive, the struggle to do something
so perfect no one will ever know.

Kamikaze.

No wonder he loved their deaths in the war.
All that duty turned into loss. No wonder
he wonders at his garden as the wind
carves it into the shapes
that do not matter, a kind of chaos,
perfection
being the one thing the wind does not know,
just as ice does not know it is only in the eye of a fish
another form of sky.

Winter 22

There is almost no air left
in the white balloon blowing across the snow.
It is wrinkled and barely lifts from the drifts.
If you could read the crinkled writing on its side
it would say: *Save the Whales,*
a temporary greed he loves,
the wish to preserve without regret.
He loves it in the way he loves
all those old poems about Byzantium,
cages full of gilded mechanical birds,
that impossible dream of beauty
while everything blows away.

Winter 23

He imagines a horse walking in snow,
consuming time
on the perimeter, going from post to post
wondering if the wire
will have fallen this time around.
That is what patience is, dumb beasts
repeating the random, going
in the direction of the greatest resistance
without even hope to guide them. It is why
he has to imagine magpies on the fenceposts,
hungry, knowing the flesh is
its own cage, insisting on it, demanding
a solution to all this dumb dreaming.

Winter 24

Just as a woman when she is brooding upon solitude
turns to winter as a metaphor for loss,
so stories are made up of missing parts
which is where all the terror comes from,
the child pleading for just a little more
before it is time to be left alone in the night
with that shape behind the door. It is someone
leaving, someone calling out, as if the words,
Go to sleep, were an answer,
as if a child and a woman in separate rooms
were exactly the same, both of them waiting
for whatever is going to be inevitable.

Winter 25

The hoarfrost on the trees is a beauty
fog leaves when it is at last consumed
by cold, obscurity transformed into light,
the bright world the heart knows upon waking.
How little it remembers of night, the fallen
animal singing as the wheels broke its flesh
on a road whose one colour was white, there being
no hesitation after the act, but to be driven
down that road believing in destiny, the confluence
of lives, animals crossing in the night.
Or the dream he remembers of his hands,
their touching innocence
knowing what they held as it cried
would never forget.
That is what is in the word *never.*
Transgression because beauty loves itself too much.
Transformation because there is nothing else to do
after the crime is committed
but shine.

Winter 26

A kind of fragile wanting as the body is
when it is too old to move without pain, desire
when the other is long gone. It is relief
from song, the same that lovers know
when they are born again, belief
when the spirit is at last made flesh.
It is the *after* as song is after singing
when the tongue makes other sound. It is
the wanting the old remember that the young
do not know, the outcry
as someone we do not know
moves toward us, the mouth making
a sound we've never heard before,
wide open, taking it all in.

Winter 27

When the wind blows it blows without regret,
invisible as the lean heart telling riddles
in the dark. It is tradition,
dumb form waiting to be filled up.
Look at the way he shovels the snow
knowing behind him the wind begins again
to worship the empty. See where he finds a leaf,
the beautiful veins, dessicated, worn fragile
as a ring upon the hand of a woman
who has turned it into a fine lament.
Everything is so thin, a leaf, a thought:
that moment in *Kings* when the woman lies with the leper
and he is not made whole. Everything
a kind of famine. Everything
diseased.

Winter 28

He lies with her in bed, the moonlight
falling through the window. It falls
upon all fours, stunned by its arrival in a place
alien to the idea of light, hunched there in a square
upon the floor. The woman beside him dreams anything,
revenge, the sound of ice in the wind, mercy,
that most intangible of songs. The picture
she has in her mind is of children
building a man out of snow.

The light trembles
as he stands to pull the curtain.
He knows passion is only distance. That is how
she described it when she described the picture
in her mind. Her version was of time,
children in a chinook, watching what had been made
melt into nothing at all, the wind
destroying everything the cold made possible.

Winter 29

There are boxes over the roses and delphiniums,
plants too tender to survive in this brutal cold.
This is the place of nurturing, the rose
because it resembles the unfolding we call love,
delphiniums because of the temple in the rock
and the oracle singing her enigmas
as she tricked men into giving up their treasure
only to find death. How they struggled to arrive
at this place, prostrating themselves, unwilling
to believe in betrayal, giving themselves to it
in the certainty there was only one answer.
That is why he moves the boxes slightly as he passes,
the living things in his garden believing
his touch is the beginning of warmth, the moment
of fecundity, the wanton madness of birth;
in this season of cold a possible temptation,
the somnolent world so willing
to believe in destiny, so willing
to believe in a beginning that has no end.

Winter 30

The brightness around him in the garden
where he stands with his hands outstretched
to the sparrows. They descend to the rich grain
he holds, quarrelling among his fingers, pecking each
other, especially the crippled one who lifts away
from their beaks and flutters in the air
just above their greed. The cold
climbs into her as they drive her into the trees.

This is what God must have felt
on the eighth day, he thinks, cruelty
everywhere around him, the omnipotence of knowing,
feeding even the least of his creatures, listening
to a bird as it dies
give itself to song in a garden
he has made out of snow.

Winter 31

What the child finds in snow is what a ship finds
in the sea, a wake left behind, a froth
that sinks back into itself, everyone else
waiting for the return, the full hold,
the grain come again, the hosannas
which are prayers to plenty. The child knows
nothing of this. He has been sent out to play
and has discovered misery.

He is learning that the footsteps he finds in snow
are his and his alone. How sweet his lament,
this silence in the negative world of cold.
It is a kind of perfect mutiny, everyone waiting
and him knowing there will be no return.
If he were a priest he would say:
This is the end of the first lesson.

Winter 32

He has already decided on the north.
He will die only when everyone else is suffering
the simple deprivations in the season
where the weak have no place.
That is when he will walk away from them into the snow
with nothing but a look of clarity
on his thin ascetic face.

This is what they will remember.

This is what they will carve
in the months when the moon
is named *starvation*, named *suffering*.
All those ghosts climbing out of their heads
when the food is gone, wondering
why the stone changes into the shapes
their hands make, white creatures that live
only now at the end of things.

Winter 33

The brightness which is the light seen from a tomb
and which is what the dead see when they gaze
with their marble eyes from the dark rooms they are
laid in. This is a whole city this snow.

Winter 34

If the word *companion* is made out of the idea of bread,
the ritual of sharing, the gift given
when there is only enough for one, is *absence*
the idea of cold? Is the space in the room
where the tree was decorated for worship
only a configuration, a chemical
map in the mind, something there that is not?

No wonder Cassandra came from a warm place.

No wonder no one believed her.

Winter 35

One is about the man who walks out into the storm
and is never seen again. We all know that one.
It is the story about grief and music,
where all the dancing is an escape
from virtue, everyone shaken by a higher crime,
the emptiness that follows completion,
the one the body knows
in the formal gentleness of suffering, everything gone,
everything forgiven in the land East of Eden.

Then there is the other story, the one
where the man enters out of the storm,
ice melting from his beard, his huge hands
moving over the fire, the fear of what will follow,
the women quiet, filling his cup and bowl
with all the food there is in hope it will be
enough, in hope he will be satisfied only with that,
and knowing he won't, knowing
this is the part of the story the reader will call
the middle, and hoping for an alternative, another
beginning, and ending it
before the mind reaches the end
with everyone crying out, everyone
saying things like: *Lie down in sorrow!*
or: *This is the burden of Babylon!*

There is another story, there always is.
The one about . . .
Of course, of course.
How cold it is with only a lamp in this small room.

Winter 36

He has arrived at a possible solution.
He will create himself in the image of a woman.
He decides upon his sister. She
is the only one who can guarantee a future
precise as the past.

He sees himself inside a body that resembles
his own, the forms of himself progressively
weaker and weaker, each version fading
into a line of translations
that are always the same text.

What a world where everything is itself.
He writes: *Dear Sister*, knowing
she knows their flesh is a repetition
of their flesh, as all snowflakes are
immaculate variations of the one original snowflake,
a shape taking shape in the cold night.
He signs his letter: *love*.

Winter 37

There are many possibilities and all of them
are endings. Each one is parallel
to the other, each one a fidelity,
a pleasure that closes the eyes
when the blood rushes away from the senses
to digest whatever has been eaten. Look
how the branches shake in the trees as the wind
rises out of the west, driving the warm air before it.
Look how the snow is released from its tension
only to find another, a shape it didn't know
it was. Look at the child in the gutter
making the corner of First and Twenty-Sixth
the confluence of The White Nile and The Blue.
See how he takes a stick and changes
the directions forever. Can you hear the people
starving to death on the Delta? Can you
see the bloated bodies as the vultures land
upon them, the featherless necks
entering their anuses, the beaks tearing
the delicate flesh? How powerful the boy is
as he watches the temples empty, the priests
lamenting this end that is of all endings
one they never imagined. How painful spring is.
How impossible this snow.

Winter 38

The scavengers have arrived
at last, the crows, returned,
having feasted on the remains
of animals he has only read
about in *Life*, the naked
opossum, the gila monster,
jewelled with poison, the
sidewinder and the mockingbird.

They are here for the season
of birth, and the snow, knowing
desire, releases the bodies
it has preserved for them in ice.

The yearlings bend forward in praise,
their black wings spread in obeisance.
The older males
climb upon them
spraying glaucous seed into their bodies
as the females circle the sky.

These are the bright cries
he hears, the abrupt terror
of greed in the moment of innocence,
a light turned off, a curtain
drawn against the bright
sickness of the sun.

Winter 39

In the north where everything that is ancient
is only in the mind, he creates his own lost city
and dresses it in flesh. It walks away from the sun
toward a frozen sea in whose name
all the letters are silent, the *a* in beauty,
the *e* in love, the *w* in snow.

Winter 40

She is a northern woman, barely more
than a child, one who has walked through the drifts
to find her dream vision. Her eyes are
covered by a blade of bone, a thin slit
cut in it so the light does not blind her.
The man she has found is not one of the four
possibilities: father, brother, lover, son.
He is the dream man, given to her by the snow.

He has wandered far from the sea,
his crew dead, his ship broken in the ice.
If there were someone there to translate his song
it would start with the words: *At last.*
But only she is there.
As he sings she cuts off his fingers,
only these small bones and the twenty-six
teeth for her necklace.

They will be her medicine, something
to shake over the bellies of women
in childbirth, the heads of men
who have returned empty from hunting,
their minds become snow.

How like a real man he is, she thinks.
How real this dream, the blood on the ice.
How thin he is, how much like the snow is his flesh.

Winter 41

Being on a journey without knowing
you are on a journey is to understand grace,
which is what he is doing
with the glass globe full of snow.
In it a small child is perpetually going nowhere,
one foot permanently anchored to the ice,
the other out there trying to go.
When spring comes it will be all that is
left of what he wants to remember of winter:
piety, because everything is weary in the rain.
A certain grief, that is what he will have.
That is what is in there, the furious snow
swirling whenever he shakes it.

Winter 42

It comes after the return, after
everything has been won and the body
feasts. It comes just after that.
That is what the story is all about,
the crashing through the door,
the shouts, the lamentation after
when the hero leaves all his dead behind
to find anything that terrible.

Winter 43

He remembers the wagon, the old
man with tired eyes, his thin horse dragging
cold through the summer days. The ice-pick
and the tongs. That clear cold jewel
swinging from the arm of the ice-man.
Memory. The mouth sucking with the greed
that is a child in the far past, a child
who is imagining the man he will be,
a sharp lean hero, immaculate and alone.
Already he is practising his cool walk,
hands in pockets, his cold clean eyes
staring through all the pain there is
at nothing. The ice-man in the heat
clicking his tongs, the old horse
leaning into the leather and the chains,
the small boy watching, in his hand
a piece of ice.

Winter 44

The body of the woman in snow, naked
and drunk. Her falling, blonde and young
into the drifts. How he carried her back
cradled in his arms, saying everything
would be alright, that love and loneliness
are lies. Remembering how he hesitated
and simply stared at her.
Remembering that.

Winter 45

The man without a name who reversed his snowshoes
and walked forward, head down, shoulders hunched.
The man who climbed the mountains
in the heart of winter, crossing the pass,
heading west into the snow.

The one they followed.

The many trails he made, each one
a perfect map, a calligraphy
for those who pursued him.
His turning upon himself,
an animal born into his own making,
crossing and recrossing his tracks.

This way, this way, they would shout.

Him walking, head down, shoulders hunched, moving
toward his own quick death, his breath
breaking sharp and hard,
entering,
leaving.

Afterword

A number of these poems appeared in earlier versions in the magazines *Border Crossings* and *Prism*. Those that appeared in *Border Crossings* won the gold medal in 1989 from the National Magazine Awards. I wish to thank the editor of *Border Crossings*, Robert Enright, for his continued faith in the efficacy of poetry.

I wish to acknowledge my editor, Anne Szumigalski, whose advice led to certain changes in individual poems as well as in the overall ordering of the manuscript. Both Lorna Crozier and Sean Virgo read through this manuscript and gave me critical advice. I thank them all.

I would like to thank the Canada Council and the Saskatchewan Arts Board, both of whom at different times invested in the labour it took to write this connected series of poems. Winter is at once both symbol and metaphor, unique and ubiquitous. Alden Nowlan said once that we live in a country where to simply go outside is to die. I agree. As I say in the poem "Winter 20," it is:

> The answer to the question:
> *But what does it mean?*
> The old Eskimo laughing at such a strange request.

Patrick Lane

Well-known Canadian poet, Patrick Lane has published extensively during a career that spans more than thirty years. His thirteen adult poetry collections include *Poems, New and Selected* (Oxford, 1978), *The Measure* (Black Moss, 1980), *Old Mother* (Oxford, 1981), *A Linen Crow, A Caftan Magpie* (Thistledown, 1985), and *Selected Poems* (Oxford, 1987). His first book for children, *Milford & Me* was published by Coteau Books in 1989.

His poetry has appeared in most major journals in Canada and the U.S., with additional publication in Europe, Asia and South America. His work has also been published in several Canadian anthologies, including, *A Sudden Radiance* (Coteau Books, 1987).

During his writing career, Patrick has won several prestigious literary awards. In 1979, he won the Governor General's Award for poetry, for *Poems, New and Selected. Selected Poems* won the Canadian Authors Association award for poetry in 1988. In 1989 a series of the winter poems from this collection (originally published in *Border Crossings*) won a Gold for poetry in the National Magazine Awards. He has also been the recipient of several senior Canada Council writing grants.

A native of British Columbia, Patrick has spent most of the 1980s in Saskatchewan either writing or teaching. He currently resides in Saskatoon with poet Lorna Crozier.

More Titles from Coteau Books

Look for other Coteau Books at your favorite bookstore. For a complete catalogue of publications—fiction, poetry, drama, criticism, non-fiction and children's literature—please write to 401 – 2206 Dewdney Avenue, Regina, Saskatchewan S4R 1H3.